ST. GEORGE'S CHAPEL

WINDSOR

ABOVE: *The Garter Service. This Thanksgiving is usually held each year in June. In the 20th century, the most notable Garter Service was probably* that of *23rd April 1948, which celebrated the six hundredth anniversary of the foundation of the Order. The Knights of the Garter, today, include* men of the highest distinction, renowned for their service to the state in war and peace. FRONT COVER: *The magnificent choir and chancel.*

ST. GEORGE'S CHAPEL

SHELAGH BOND

ST. GEORGE'S CHAPEL dominates the lower ward of Windsor Castle and for 500 years has been the home of the College of St. George and of the Order of the Garter. It is the last in a succession of chapels in the castle, of which the earliest was built in the late 11th century for the needs of the garrison, king and court. Then in 1240 Henry III ordered a chapel to be built in the lower ward, close to his new apartments. It was dedicated to St. Edward the Confessor and stood on the site of the present Albert Memorial Chapel.

Foundation and Endowment

It was Edward III, Henry III's great-grandson, who by his two foundations a century later, gave this chapel an importance far exceeding that of the usual castle chapel. Early in 1348 the king, fresh from his victories at Crécy and Calais, inaugurated the Most Noble Order of the Garter as 'a society, fellowship and college of knights'. These, 26 in number, including the sovereign, were 'to show fidelity and friendliness one towards another' and the famous blue garter was to be 'a symbol of amity'. Edward III thus linked to himself 'in the bonds of Amity and Peace' such great soldiers as the Black Prince, the Earl of Warwick and the Earl of Salisbury. The Order symbolised the new ideals of chivalry and it also helped to diminish the dangers of political disaffection. Furthermore, the splendid tournaments, yearly feasts, the opportunity of personal contact with

*   *   *

FACING PAGE: *The Nave, looking east, showing the striking panelled walls, thinly moulded arcades and rectangular lines.*

RIGHT: *The College seal, made about 1561, showing the Virgin Mary, St. George and the royal arms in a Garter.*

the sovereign—all meant that membership soon became regarded as the highest distinction.

Within seven months of inaugurating the Order, Edward III on 6th August 1348 refounded Henry III's Chapel in honour of the Virgin Mary, St. George and St. Edward and established within it a body of clergy. His purpose was to found a large-scale chantry to pray for his own salvation and that of his family and all faithful souls; and also to endow the chapel (where he had himself been baptised) to carry out this function for ever. In 1351 the Pope granted the new body exemption from the jurisdiction of the Archbishop of Canterbury and the Bishop of Salisbury (in whose diocese Windsor then lay). Thus St. George's became, and still is, a 'peculiar' and 'a royal free chapel'. Statutes in 1352 defined the membership of this 'college', a word signifying in the Middle Ages a collection of men with a common purpose, usually ecclesiastical. It was to consist of a dean or warden, 12 canons, 13 priest vicars, 4 clerks, 6 choristers, a virger and 26 alms knights.

Although the Order of the Garter is not mentioned in the foundation deed and statutes of the College, the close connection between the two bodies was made clear in the Garter statutes. The dean (or a canon) was to be Register of the Order; the clergy and poor knights (who represented the Garter Knights at daily services) were to be members of the establishment of the Order and to participate in its religious services, and the Garter Knights themselves were to have their stalls in the collegiate chapel. These connections are maintained today.

Edward III during the next ten years, at a cost of over £6,000 adapted the existing chapel for its new function and provided houses and offices for the College and Order. There was, fortunately, space to plan the new development. Henry III's residence

in the lower ward had been burnt to the ground, but his chapel remained; this formed the northern side of a quadrangle to be built round the special grass plot which had separated Henry III's chapel from his apartments. A central space, surrounded by a cloister, off which lie offices, chapel and lodgings is a familiar plan. It has been only recently discovered, however, that its first use other than in monastic houses probably occurs in Edward III's new college at Windsor.

Plague delayed the start of building works for two years. Then clerks of the works were appointed, with John de Sponlee as architect. First the chapel was refurnished as a collegiate church; choir stalls were carved, new windows were filled with painted glass and the provision of a statue of St. George underlined his supremacy as patron saint of College and Order. The builders proceeded in an anti-clockwise direction round the cloister, and on the eastern side a large chapter

Continued on page 6

3

ABOVE: *The Great West Window, containing 75 figures, mostly of the original 16th century glass. Warrior Saints, Popes and Archbishops of many centuries are depicted.*

FACING PAGE: *The Rutland chapel was the chantry of Anne, Duchess of Exeter, Edward IV's sister, and Sir Thomas St. Leger, her husband. In the centre stands the alabaster tomb of*

George Manners, 11th Lord Ros (1513), and Anne his wife. Their descendants became dukes of Rutland. Behind the tomb three of the five Beryl Dean embroideries can be seen.

house, with the dean's residence above, was quickly built, together with a vaulted vestry, which is today the dean's private chapel. To the north, on the third side, a second cloister was joined to the Dean's Cloister by a narrow passage. Here, close to the outer wall of the castle on the site of Henry III's burnt-out residence, 13 half-timbered two-storeyed houses were built, their 13 doors opening on to the walk of the Canons' Cloister, as it is called. The Canons, today three in number, still live in these houses,

which were finished for their 12 predecessors and the 13 priest vicars in July 1353. The next two years saw the erection on the west side of the Dean's Cloister of an imposing entrance to this whole collegiate area. This is the Porch of Honour which, with its beautiful vault and panelling, is regarded as one of the first examples of the use of the perpendicular style in the country. Over it was built a room to house the plate, relics, treasures and muniments of the college. This room is called the Aerary, a strange word

which occurs only at Windsor and comes direct from the Latin 'aerarium', meaning a treasury. Today it is full of the archives of the College. Finally, by 1356 the cloister arcade had been rebuilt and most of Edward III's great building works were complete.

The endowment needed to maintain the college was considerable; and within three years of the foundation eleven churches had been given to the chapter, together with an annual sum of a hundred marks (£66·67) from the borough of Northampton. In 1352 came the most unusual grant of all—that of a last of red herrings, at least 10,000 fish, to come each year from the bailiffs of Yarmouth. It has been suggested that this was a penance imposed on the town for the murder of one of its magistrates; and the herrings continued to be sent, with no little trouble, until Queen Anne's reign. John, Duke of Bedford, was responsible in 1421 for a grant of lavish proportions—property which had belonged to the alien priories in England dependent on the famous abbey of Bec. Then in 1475 Edward IV began to build a new and magnificent chapel, the present St. George's. He also refounded the college, bestowing on it a charter of incorporation, and between 1474 and 1483 there were granted no fewer than 8 churches, 14 manors, St. Anthony's Hospital in London, 2 priories and other lands.

At the Reformation, therefore, St. George's had become, by these and other lesser gifts, the third richest ecclesiastical foundation in the country, second only to Westminster Abbey and Canterbury Cathedral—a situation due in part to Henry VIII's own generosity. Wishing to be buried at Windsor he left the college, in his will, property to the yearly value of £600 for masses, obits, sermons and alms after his death. St. George's was able to maintain itself, with varying degrees of comfort, from these endowments until 1867. Then, as part of a nationwide redistribution of the resources of the Church of England, the chapter surrendered its landed property to the Ecclesiastical Commissioners for an annual sum of money. This surrender ended a 500-year old tradition of property administration which by then covered over 200 parishes in some thirty counties in England and Wales. As the annual sum has at no time been increased, it is small wonder that the

Life in the Middle Ages

Soon after 1348 the first dean, John de la Chambre, and twelve canons were appointed, and the chapters of the next two centuries contained many who were outstanding in both church and state. Medieval government was largely in the hands of clergy and so it was usual for the king to recompense service with preferment in the church. St. George's lay only a minute away from the king when he was in residence at Windsor and its clergy could there-

college still needs benefactors today and that the Society of the Friends of St. George's has been founded for this purpose.

*   *   *

FACING PAGE: *The beautiful white marble monument to Princess Charlotte, daughter of George IV, who tragically died in child-birth in 1817.*

ABOVE: *The tomb of George V and Queen Mary. Designed by Sir Edwin Lutyens, the sarcophagus stands at the north west corner of the nave. The effigies are of bianca del mare stone, and were the work of Sir William Reid Dick.*

fore easily play this dual role. Walter Almaly, for example, was dean from 1381 to 1389 and also a successful king's clerk, as was Richard Kingston, dean from 1402 to 1418; and many canons held similar posts. Richard Metford, canon from 1375 to 1390, was one of the ablest members of these medieval chapters. He was a close servant of Richard II, his keeper of the secret seal and also the first Windsor canon to become a bishop, being consecrated to Chichester in 1390. Cardinal Wolsey is probably the outstanding example of a Windsor canon combining his clerical duties with those of a minister of state.

Continual worship was, however, the purpose of the Windsor foundation; as at other collegiate churches there was a sequence of daily services from dawn to dusk. Two attendance registers, preserved in the Aerary, are an impressive reminder of this daily obligation. The dean and canons attended at least one of the greater services on many days in the year; the poor knights were present three times a day with considerable regularity. Eight noughts are crammed into the daily column opposite each priest

vicar's name; each of them almost invariably attended all eight services.

Considerable magnificence surrounded the performance of this *opus Dei*, God's work, at Windsor. Medieval inventories list a profusion of glittering vestments, such as the golden cope ornamented with the martyrdoms of various saints, given by the Black Prince; and the vestments, copes and altar hangings of cloth of gold powdered with birds which had been contrived out of the wedding gown of Joan, Countess of Kent. No less brilliant were the chalices, crosses, censers, pyxes and other ornaments of precious metal, enriched with jewels, which made Windsor's treasures not far inferior to those of Canterbury. At great festivals the richest ornaments were displayed on the high altar and the most important relics carried in procession. The Cross Gneth, given by Edward III, was foremost among these, being a relic of the true cross of Calvary, which had been the national palladium of Wales in the 13th century until its capture by Edward I in 1283. Another relic, the heart of St. George, had been fittingly given by the Emperor Sigismund when he attended

7

the Feast of the Garter in 1416, at which he was chosen a companion of the order.

Splendid music accompanied the services. For some time after the foundation, choral music was pre-eminent, and organs were little used, no organist being named in the statutes. Music, indeed, played an important part and three canons, John Aleyn, Thomas Danet and Richard Wyot, were well-known composers. During the 15th century, as plainsong began to yield to polyphonic music demanding more voices, the number of clerks, or singingmen, rose from 4 to 13 between 1476 and 1490. And at this time when England was leading Europe in music, it is significant that no fewer than four of the five most important books of music to survive in the country from this period, came from Windsor.

To countless devout Englishmen, however, in the latter years of the 15th century, St. George's ranked as one of the great centres of pilgrimage in the country. Valuable relics were already among its treasures. In 1481, the body of Master John Schorn was re-buried in the recently built south east corner of the new St. George's, now known as the Lincoln Chapel. He had been rector of North Marston in Buckinghamshire until his death in 1314, since when his reputation for effecting cures, especially for ague, had flourished. Pilgrims in their thousands followed him to St. George's. In 1484, the body of the saintly Henry VI was brought from Chertsey and re-buried a few yards to the west of John Schorn. This even further enhanced the popularity of St. George's as a place of pilgrimage, alms were placed in the money box which still stands by the tomb and votive offerings were hung round the shrine.

Within the new chapel, many chantries were founded, for during the 15th century persons of wealth

*   *   *

FACING PAGE: *The Nave, facing west, with its lierne vaulting, was finished in 1509. The large aisle and clerestory windows flood the nave with light.*

RIGHT: *This alabaster tablet in the Bray Chapel contains the bust of Dean Giles Tomson, as Bishop of Gloucester. The shell niche and the cherubs are typical Renaissance features.*

often made such provision for continued prayers after their death. One or two priests were appointed to sing (*cantare*) mass and daily office was to be said for ever at a special altar. Between 1475 and 1522 nine chantries were founded at St. George's, among them those of Edward IV, Christopher Urswick, dean 1496–1505, Lord Hastings and Anne, Duchess of Exeter.

Life in the Later Centuries

As elsewhere the Reformation brought great changes to Windsor. In spite, however, of the destruction and sale of the medieval treasures of the chapel, the plate, vestments and relics, and the altered pattern of worship, there was, fortunately, no essential break with the past as the College survived intact, its statutes unimpaired and its chantries exempt from suppression.

The Windsor musical tradition never faltered. John Marbeck, organist from about 1541 until his death in

1585 was one of the members of the college whose life at St. George's spanned these unsettled years. He is regarded as perhaps the most famous of the chapel's musicians and his setting of the first English liturgy, published in 1550, is still widely used today. He was followed as organist by Nathaniel Giles, who held the post from 1585 until 1632, and it was during his tenure that Frederick, Duke of Würtemberg, on Sunday 20th August 1592, visited the chapel and noted afterwards that 'the music and especially the organ was very fine . . . a small boy sang so beautifully that it was wonderful to listen to him'. Giles was succeeded by William Child, who was organist, except during the Commonwealth period, until his death in 1697. There can be few

churches to have had only three organists between 1541 and 1697, a period of 156 years. The diarist Samuel Pepys, who was a friend of Child, noted appreciatively after his visit in 1666 that there was 'a good choir of voices', a tribute reflected still more warmly in the verses on the organist's tomb near the organ loft:

> 'How fit in Heavenlie Choirs to beare thy part Before well practised in the sacred art.'

Child's years at Windsor had been interrupted by the Civil War, for from 1643 to 1660 the life of St. George's came virtually to a standstill—its only break in over 600 years. With the exception of the poor knights, members of the college were evicted, established services were no longer held and chapter properties were

redistributed. Apart from this interlude, however, the 17th century was in many ways one of the most remarkable in Windsor's history. During this time enrichment of worship began to return. New altar plate, commissioned in 1631 from the Dutch goldsmith Christian
Continued on page 14

*　　　*　　　*

ABOVE: *The Bray chapel. Sir Reginald Bray, K.G., who died in 1503, was one of the great benefactors of St. George's Chapel.*

FACING PAGE: *The Beaufort chapel, which contains the tomb of Charles Somerset, the 1st Earl of Worcester of the new creation, (d. 1526) and his wife Elizabeth (d. 1514). The unusual grille was made by Jan van den Einde.*

The Choir

The Choir *(left)* and chancel, begun in 1475, were finished by 1484. Records exist of the construction and the names of the actual carvers and the amounts they were paid. The head carver was William Berkeley. Along the desk fronts of the stalls the words of the 20th and 84th psalms are engraved in beautiful lettering, and on the backs of the stalls are carvings of various subjects. The vault was made by John Hylmer and William Vertue between 1506 and 1509. Each knight's achievements hang over his stall—his sword, helmet, mantling, crest and banner. In the centre of the choir are buried Henry VIII, Jane Seymour, Charles I and a child of Queen Anne. William Child, organist from 1632 to 1697, gave the black and white marble floor.

The Sovereign's stall *(above)* shows much of the detail and intricacy with which the woodwork in St. George's was carved, between 1478 and 1484. The canopy is by Henry Emlyn (1787). The other stalls on the south side are usually of foreign knights. The diamond-shaped stall plate, for instance, is that of Charles the Bold, Duke of Burgundy (1468). Above are statues of St. Edmund and St. Edward.

canon from 1606 and Bishop of Rochester from 1611, overlapping at Windsor with Giles Tomson, Dean and Bishop, who was one of the translators of the Authorised Version of the Bible. Ralph Brideoake, canon from the Restoration until 1678, was also Bishop of Chichester. Other canons such as Richard Field, Richard Montague and Godfrey Goodman were learned theologians, influencing the thought of the church. David Stokes, Montague's son-in-law, was a fellow of Eton College and canon, except during the Commonwealth, from 1628 until 1669. From his tombstone in the ambulatory we learn that he knew Latin, Greek, Hebrew, Chaldaic, Arabic and Syriac. 'Since you have learnt so many languages in so short a time' says his latin epitaph . 'you will now easily be able to learn the tongue of angels': a charming tribute to a scholar and linguist.

The music, learning and distinction of St. George's in the 17th century may in some measure have been due to the attractions which the chapel offered to the ablest clergy and musicians when the sovereign and court were spending long periods at the castle, thus making Windsor the centre of affairs. This largely ceased with Queen Anne's death in 1714 and for the next fifty years few of the 12 canons stayed at Windsor for more than the minimum period each year, chapter meetings were perfunctory and the chapel fell into disrepair. Then during the 1770's George III and his family began to live at Windsor again and one of the most remarkable results of his devotion to the castle and his lengthy residence was the restoration of St. George's. It was 'perhaps the first in the world for beauty and splendour, but dirty and disregarded to such a degree as to become a nuisance to the eye . . . and the pavement of this royal chapel would be

Van Vianen, did not survive the depredations of the Commonwealth, but after the Restoration further elaborate plate was quickly purchased and given, and is still in use today. It includes a chalice, given by Lady Mary Heveningham, the wealthy wife of the regicide, who was himself imprisoned a few hundred yards away in the castle from 1660 to 1678. Celebrations of the Order of the Garter were held, lasting for three days, each with its appropriate services and processions—

'pompous solemnities' according to the antiquary Ashmole, who as Windsor Herald took part in them— but probably they were among the most elaborate ceremonies known to the English church since the close of the Middle Ages.

At this time too, the chapter contained men of note. Some were translated to bishoprics, among them, for example, John Buckeridge, President of St. John's College, Oxford, and tutor to William Laud. He was a

*   *   *

LEFT: *Fixed to the back of each stall are metallic plates, bearing the arms of Knights of the Garter, some 700 in all. Those in the centre which are cut to the shape of the heraldic design date from the 1420's and are some of the finest in the Chapel.*

FACING PAGE: *The High Altar. Much of the plate dates from Charles II's reign, but the foremost dish is Elizabethan. The altar cloth was made for Queen Victoria's Golden Jubilee.*

KING HENRY. VI
1422-1471

Jnundie fanbus : haeenfa patenter beudi :
Juftat et amdet : ftephanū plebs impia iuftū :

disgraceful to a barn'—according to a description in the *Gentleman's Magazine*, by the son of a former organist. Though disloyal and outspoken,

*   *   *

FACING PAGE: *Henry VI's tomb. Edward IV was buried on the left of the High Altar and the oriels above form part of his chantry chapel.*

ABOVE, left: *Edward III, Founder of the College of St. George and of the Order of the Garter, is holding the orb, with an open crown on his head and the crowns of Scotland and France encircling his sword.*

ABOVE, right: *The Hastings chantry chapel is decorated with contemporary paintings from the life of St. Stephen.*

indeed, he was presumably well-informed. Between 1782 and 1792 over £21,000, given mainly by the king himself, was spent on St. George's. The work was entrusted to the oversight of Henry Emlyn, an able local architect and craftsman. He repaired pavements, stonework and woodwork. He added choir stalls, carving and appropriate detail with such skill that his work can scarcely be distinguished from the medieval. He designed the present organ gallery, in Coade's artificial stone which that arbiter of neo-gothic taste, Horace Walpole, praised as 'airy and harmonious'; and he redesigned Edward IV's upper chantry as a comfortable room for regular use by his royal patron on Sundays.

The altered circumstances of the 19th century brought change to St. George's as to so many of the nation's institutions. The resources of the church had to be redeployed in the rapidly growing industrial towns, and the Cathedrals Act of 1840 provided for the suspension at Windsor of no fewer than 8 of the 12 canonries as they fell vacant; followed by a similar reduction in the number of minor canons from 7 to 4 by an Order in Council of 1849. In 1867 St. George's, in addition, surrendered all its landed property for a fixed annual sum of money.

A smaller chapter and a poorer college—but no diminution of influence, for the Victorian era saw the castle again at the centre of affairs.

The Queen divided her time between Windsor, Osborne and Balmoral more or less equally, but since the Prince Consort's death the castle had had a special significance for her. One of her most trusted advisers, Gerald Wellesley, was dean for 28 years and from 1854 when, having refused a bishopric, he moved to Windsor until his death in 1882, his counsel in family and ecclesiastical matters was constantly sought. He also exercised, as a life-long friend of Gladstone, a certain amount of political influence and it is not surprising that at his death the Queen should lament: 'Windsor without him will be strange and dreadful.'

During these years, too, many of the Military Knights (whose name had been changed from that of Poor Knights in 1833 by William IV) were distinguished soldiers. They had fought in the Peninsular War, at Waterloo, in China, India, and the Crimea and their gallantry made them fitting representatives of the Garter Knights in the chapel. Their presence within a primarily ecclesiastical college also gave, as it has always done, a special quality to the life of the lower ward.

The 19th century saw many canons holding their stalls for a considerable number of years; for example C. L. Courtenay, an early follower of the Oxford Movement, was at Windsor from 1859 to 1894. He overlapped for part of the time with Lord Wriothesley Russell, canon from 1840 to 1886, a strong Evangelical (these Victorian chapters represented no exclusive church party) and Frederick Anson, whose especial concern was care for the fabric, was there from

*   *   *

ABOVE LEFT: *King George VI Memorial Chapel in the north choir aisle was dedicated in 1969. The king's body rests under the black ledger stone.*

LEFT: *The Lincoln Tomb. The Earl of Lincoln was Lord High Admiral of England. He died in 1585 and his effigy depicts him in armour, with a greyhound at his feet. His wife Elizabeth Fitzgerald has the Fitzgerald ape at her feet.*

FACING PAGE: *The north choir aisle. The fan vaulting was added in Henry VII's reign and the two most easterly bays are lower, because of Edward IV's two-storeyed chantry. On the right is the Hastings chantry chapel.*

and laity can meet to discuss contemporary problems—a 20th century attempt to re-interpret the work of the college in modern terms, alongside the continuing daily Eucharist and Offices of the chapel.

The Chapel

The building of St. George's Chapel, together with those of Eton College, King's College, Cambridge and Henry VII at Westminster, had formed a climax of achievement at the very close of the Middle Ages, when the perpendicular style, that uniquely English contribution to the architecture of Europe, reached its peak. St. George's, though frequently restored in the course of its subsequent history has remained much as its designers intended it, and the masons and carvers who worked on it from 1475 to 1528 preserved the unity of the original concept.

Viewed from the outside St. George's is almost symmetrical, the nave and chancel being of six and seven bays. Polygonal chapels extend from the central transepts; and each end of both west and south fronts terminates in similarly balancing and protruding chapels. Elaborate parapets rise over the aisle and clerestory windows, and both the buttresses of the aisles and the flying buttresses of the nave end in pinnacles. It is features such as these, needed for stability, which nonetheless give to gothic buildings their special grace and life. On the pinnacles stand a series of strange beasts, each 4 ft. 6 ins. tall, which were erected in 1930 to replace the originals which Sir Christopher Wren had ordered to be removed for safety in the 17th century. These beasts, or royal supporters, trace the Tudor descent from Edward

1845 until 1885. In recent times one of the longest tenures was that of Canon J. N. Dalton who was at Windsor for nearly half a century. He had been tutor to Prince Edward and Prince George (later George V) from 1871 to 1885 and then for the rest of his life, from 1885 until 1931, he was probably the most strong-minded and active canon in the chapter. He was responsible for converting the choir school, which had catered for the choristers' education from Edward III's reign, into a preparatory school taking other boarders and day boys; he catalogued thousands of documents in the college archives; and he was

foremost in organising and seeing to a triumphant conclusion the Restoration of 1920–30.

The last half century has seen activity in many fields—in historical research under the initiative of the late Canon S. L. Ollard; in music where organists have enhanced Windsor's reputation and where Edmund Fellowes gained international renown for his work on Tudor Church music; and in further restoration work in the Deanery, Canons' houses and Chapter Library. Most recently St. George's House, in the precincts, has been established as a conference centre where clergy

*   *   *

FACING PAGE: *The Albert Memorial Chapel was the one built by Henry III and adapted by Edward III as the first chapel of the College and the Order. Between 1863 and 1873 Queen Victoria converted this into a chapel in memory of the Prince Consort. The chapel is a remarkable example of Victorian workmanship.*

ABOVE: *Henry III's 13th-century door bears its original elegant ironwork, signed by the smith, Gilebertus.*

III through the houses of Lancaster and York. Henry VI was buried on the south, Edward IV on the north, of the high altar. The beasts follow a similar arrangement; on the south are the lion, unicorn, swan, antelope, panther, yale and red dragon of Lancaster; and on the north the falcon, hart, bull, black dragon, white lion, hind and greyhound of York. The two families of beasts are mingled on the transepts.

The west front is typically English, featuring a small doorway with a huge window so that the nave has as much light as possible. Above the window, three niches contain statues of the Virgin and Child, St. George with the dragon and Edward the Confessor—the triple dedication of the chapel.

They are of Coade's artificial stone and were erected in 1799 to the design of John Bacon. Until 1872, when the ceremonial staircase was added to the west end, the main entrance to the chapel was by the south door. This south 'show front', designed to impress, is more elaborate than the north side. For example, window mouldings are more complex and the buttresses, unlike those of the north, which are plain, contain niches with statues. They depict eleven benefactors of the chapel and were erected as late as 1882 as replacements of earlier statues. Also of 19th century date are many of the gargoyles all round the chapel, which, with their grotesque carving and lively caricatures perfectly catch the medieval

spirit. On the north and south walls are examples of the royal badge of Edward IV, builder of the chapel—a rose, surrounded by two circles of petals, with a crucifix in the centre.

Inside St. George's, the nave gives an impression of light, space and uniformity. The arches are everywhere flattened and four-centred, the walls are panelled regularly and the mullions and transoms of the windows are arranged in a gridiron pattern. At clerestory level in nave, choir and chapels alike, runs a frieze of winged angels, charmingly breaking the monotony of these rectangular lines. Dominating the nave is the great west window, containing 75 principal lights of which 60 are filled with early 16th century glass. They depict 24 popes, 29 kings, princes and warriors, 8 archbishops, 2 bishops, 10 saints and two civilians. One of these is a mason, almost certainly William Vertue, who was responsible for building the vault. He stands, carrying his hammer and chisel, dressed in fine robes and a cap and wearing the blunt-toed shoes of Henry VIII's reign. With its large windows, panelled walls, thinly moulded arcades and rectangular lines the nave is typical of the perpendicular style at its latest and perhaps most serene.

The vault is of the type known as lierne, and was recently called 'the marvel of the chapel'. Down the centre, from the east end of the choir right to the west window, runs a central ridge rib, broken only by the crossing. This is flanked by a straight longitudinal rib on each side. This central flat ceiling area is arranged with further small ribs to form stars

*   *   *

and is adorned with elaborate, gaily coloured bosses. Among these can be seen the Beaufort portcullis, the Tudor rose and the hemp brake of Sir Reginald Bray. To each side of this central 'ceiling' is a coved area, only slightly less flat, with 13 slender palm frond ribs springing from the arcade. In the choir vault, built slightly later, the contract bearing the date of 5th June 1506, the pattern is similar but more varied, for elaborate central pendants alternate with the bosses. Over the crossing itself is a fan vault, with the cones meeting, but not overlapping at the sides; and in the centre a large boss contains the arms of Henry VIII with the date 1528, when the last stone was inserted. The choir aisles are also fan vaulted, in a style reminiscent of Sherborne Abbey and the south porch of Burford Church: no coincidence, for the latter was by the hand of Henry Jennings the master mason who worked at Windsor.

The nave was designed to give space for magnificent processions, for con-

courses of pilgrims and for preaching; the choir had to accommodate the college at daily services. To walk under the organ screen from the nave into the choir is to pass from light and space into a dark and richly coloured enclosure. It is the combination of polished wood, gleaming stall plates and brilliant knightly achievements which gives the choir its unique appearance. The choir stalls themselves were carved mainly between 1478 and 1485 of Windsor oak, under the direction of William Berkeley, the chief carver. In the course of George III's restoration of the chapel Henry Emlyn repaired damaged work and also added new desks and stalls: the king's sons were all made Knights of the Garter and more accommodation was needed. The hundreds of scenes and details are full of variety and humour. Some of the finials of the bench ends record the lives of St. George and Edward III. In the sovereign's stall the misericord shows the meeting at Picquigny of Edward IV and Louis XI; and one of Emlyn's additions records George III and the queen driving to St. Paul's in a coach for a thanksgiving service on the occasion of his recovery in 1789.

On the back of each stall are fixed

the stall plates of the Knights of the Garter: 'a heraldic storehouse of the highest artistic excellence, unequalled in Europe'. From the foundation of the Order in 1348 to the present day each knight has had a plate, bearing his arms, fixed to his stall. Some have disappeared and only 90 survive from the old chapel but there are still some 700, the earliest being that of Ralph, Lord Bassett, who was a knight from 1368 to 1390. Above the stall of each present knight, hangs his mantling, surmounted by helmet and crest, with sword and banner above.

The choir is obviously the centre and climax of St. George's Chapel. Here daily offices have been said or sung, the Eucharist celebrated and ceremonies such as royal funerals, weddings and Garter installations have taken place for 500 years. Thus the choir epitomises a continuous life, marked by powers of adaptation, which have enabled the College to contribute to the life of church and state from 1348 to the present day.

*   *   *

ABOVE: *The south 'show front', with its three polygonal chantry chapels, as seen from Henry VIII's Gateway.*

ACKNOWLEDGEMENTS

Photographs are by Sydney W. Newbery, Hon. FIIP, FRPS and Gerald Newbery, FIIP, FRPS, excepting: pp i, 3, 12, 13, 18 (above), 23 (above), A. F. Kersting, FIIP, FRPS; p 1, Reginald Davis, FIIP, FRPS; p 23 (below), Godfrey Argent.

SBN 85372 013 4